THE GOLDEN BOOK
OF
PASSION

By

Father John Doe

(Rev. Ralph Pfau)

Author

of

Sobriety and Beyond

Sobriety Without End

* * *

The SMT Guild, Inc.
P.O. Box 313
Indianapolis, IN 46206

Hazelden Publishing
Center City, Minnesota 55012-0176
hazelden.org/bookstore

© 1960 by Hazelden Foundation.
First published 1960
by SMT Guild, Inc., Indianapolis.
First published by Hazelden 1998

All rights reserved
Printed in the United States of America
No portion of this publication may be reproduced in any manner
without the written permission of the publisher

ISBN: 978-1-56838-334-7

"Blessed is the man that endureth temptation; for when he hath been proven, he shall receive a crown of life."[1]

PASSION—SIN

During many years of teaching and conducting question periods, this writer has been asked thousands of questions. However, of all those questions, only one could not be given a specific answer. This question was asked by a grade school student many years ago: "How can we commit a capital sin?"

To this question there can be no answer, only an explanation, for no one can possibly *commit* a capital sin—pride, anger, covetousness, lust, gluttony, envy, and sloth—for these are not sins. They only *lead* to sin. But the lad's question has made this writer feel that there are undoubtedly many, many people in this world who are quite confused by this same terminology, and are quite mixed up in their understanding of the capital sins. Down through the years, this writer has seen evidence everywhere that many, many people are confused and mixed up about a lot of things because they are mixed up and confused about the terminology used to describe certain things.

The word *sin* is one such confusing term. Even in its generalized connotation, we find very many misunderstandings about the term itself. Particularly do we find this misunderstanding when *feeling* enters the picture when, actually, feeling has nothing to do with sin. No matter how much or how deeply we may *feel* like doing something wrong (or right), unless we freely *will* a thought, word, or action, there can be no formal sin (nor act of virtue). Only a person's *will* can sin. Sin is always in the will—and likewise, virtue is always in the will. The will is all that is really ours. Feeling may urge us to commit the most heinous crime, or it may urge us to perform the most heroic act of virtue, but unless our will acts, we have neither disintegrated morally nor have we progressed in virtue. That brings us to another frequently misunderstood term—*passion*.

Ask the average person today what passion is, and it is almost certain that they will connect sex in some way with the description. In fact, this writer believes that most people would tell you that a passionate person is one who tends very much toward sexual indulgence in any or all of its vagaries when, actually, we know that there are many passions: love, hate, fear, etc. St. Thomas Aquinas enumerated them all and analyzed each of them in a very clear manner in his very philosophical and theological treatise, *Summa Theologica*. But it is not within the scope of this volume to analyze or enumerate all passions. It is this writer's purpose only to clarify what we feel is a very widespread misunderstanding that caused the student to ask the question about committing capital sin. In doing so, this writer hopes to analyze, clarify, and classify these capital sins and thus get a better understanding of two things: the precise part that passion, feeling, and sin play in relation to life and our fallen human nature; and the impact of these so-called capital sins on every action of our lives—conscious and otherwise.

We use the term *so-called* designedly, because we think that the very labels *capital* and *sin* are misleading. It may be true that with an accurate understanding of the original terms, they are named very appropriately. But this writer feels that, over the years, these words have taken on an entirely different meaning from their original sense, and as a result many, many people have become very confused as to the actual meaning of the term *capital sins*.

The word *capital* originally was taken from the Latin word *caput* (plural *capita*), which literally means "head" or "source." So capital sins are not sins, but *sources* of sin. The original Latin was written *capita peccati* and literally translated means "sources of sin." However, since today people look upon capital to mean the chief or the most important or primary, they also look upon the capital sins as being the chief or most important ones versus simply tagging them as a source of sin. Think about capital cities, which are not always the biggest nor the most important, but rather the source of law and management. Or consider *caput fluminis*—the source from whence the river flows.

So it is that the capital sins are not the most important or primary sins, but they are the sources whence all sin flows: the sources of all sin. Likewise the use of the plural *sins* is also misleading. Euphonically, it deceives us into thinking it designates *actual sins* rather than merely the source of sin.

Personally, this writer has never thought the term *capital sin* an appropriate name. I like the term *passion* much better, even though passion is a broader term. I feel in modern language connotations, it makes much more sense. And this writer feels that calling them the *seven basic passions* of the human *personality* is far more accurate and understandable than calling them capital sins.

Further evidence for this preference is that the word *passion* both etymologically and definitively comes closer to specifying just exactly what these basic urges or drives or passions really are.

The term *passion* comes from the Latin word *passio*, which is the noun of the verb *patior, pati, passus sum* and means "to suffer, to put up with." What is a better description for these seven basic drives than something all humans must put up with, must suffer all of their lives!

So there we have it—the seven basic passions of man: pride, anger, covetousness, lust, gluttony, envy, and sloth. These basic drives are often very disturbing, but ones we must suffer and put up with all our lives, ever alert lest they lead us to sin, to wrongdoing, to problems of every type and kind. It is from these passions inborn in every human being that all sin—all mental, emotional, and spiritual problems—in some way or another stem. One or more of our basic passions cause or occasion all troubles, either directly or indirectly.

While all these passions lead to sin if not controlled, all are controllable presuming the grace of God. In his letter to the Romans, St. Paul referred to his own troubles with controlling these passions when he exclaimed, "for the good which I will, I do not; but the evil which I will not, that I do. . . . Unhappy man that I am, who shall deliver me . . . The Grace of God."[2]

These drives are not all equally strong in the same person; nor are they equally strong in each individual. And in every individual we always find one that is the strongest. Down through the ages, spiritual writers have advised us that if we control one, all the rest will come along. The reason for this advice is that man's soul is a simple substance and cannot be divided. For this same reason, conflict of all kinds is very devastating to the human personality.

The passions are good in themselves, and under the control of reason and will, also produce good. But because of our fallen human nature, with the will weakened and reason clouded, all of these passions tend to get out of control and go beyond reason. Then we have sin and problems and troubles. So let's take a look at these passions in order that we may the better understand them, and use and control them for a happier, holier and better adjusted life.

Although listed as the first and primary one, *pride* actually overflows into and influences or accentuates all the others. Perhaps we could diagram them as follows:

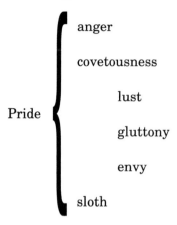

From this we can see that pride touches off all the rest. Anger overemphasizes *my rights;* covetousness overemphasizes *my things;* lust overemphasizes *my satisfaction*; gluttony overemphasizes *my body;* envy overemphasizes *my welfare and success;* and sloth overemphasizes *my comfort.*

They constantly impart pressure upon and influence our feelings, our thinking, our actions, even our willingness. These passions interact with that intricate and complicated part of the person called the nervous system—our bodily reactions, our glandular disturbances, plus certain types of thinking—to produce emotions: sadness, fear, joy, elation, etc. The word *emotion* itself comes from two Latin words: *e* and *motus*, which literally means "a movement." Emotions differ from intellectual feelings like fear and joy, in that in the emotions, the mind, body, and soul all take part including our nervous system. This is the reason that emotions can become so complicated and have such disastrous results on human personalities if they are not properly understood and controlled in their origin, and their various impacts ignored, lest analysis and/or agitated concern cause a lasting mark on the total personality through its mark on the nervous system, the glandular system, the blood vessels, the heart, or what have you. This emotional control is achieved—albeit slowly and imperfectly—by keeping these seven basic drives that all of us have and will have until we are dead within the dictates of reason and will.

Now let us analyze each other in order and try to recognize evidences of them in ourselves. And then let us try and learn what to do about them, because of all the various influences upon happiness, adjustment, and sanctity, these drives play the most important part.

PRIDE

Pride in itself is a good and necessary drive in life. Without it there would be no self-improvement; there would be no family improvement; there would be no work improvement. And so as long as pride is reasonable and justifiable, it is good. It is not wrong, therefore, to be proud of a job well done or that we are members of AA. Such realizations are both reasonable and justifiable. But when pride goes beyond the limits of reason and truth, then we have a pride that is wrong and sinful. We see such in our many refusals—to accept ourselves and our limitations, to admit our faults, to be tolerant of our neighbor—and all the thousands of other sins that come along in the wake of pride beyond reason and truth. In plain language, pride enters all those thoughts or actions that have to do with ourselves in relation to ourselves, others, or life's circumstances. Humility, the opposite of pride, is assuming "I am what I am"; pride is assuming "I am what I ain't," bringing about egotism, vanity, frustration, resentments, self-pity, and what have you.

We, therefore, define pride as "an inordinate appraisal of self." It precedes and causes all of the other extremes of passion and sin by the very fact it is based on a falsehood—a lie. It is simply us pretending to be what we are not or pretending not to be what we really are. For this reason all alcoholics have become so proud, and they have become such liars! And since "pride goeth before a fall," our falls were frequent, our problems were many, our remorse great, our guilt deep, and our repentance short-lived.

Let's take a look and see all the evidences of pride that were and are present in our great personalities.

1. *Taking all the credit.* If we listen all around us, within and without of us, we will hear the refrain: "All that I am, and all that I hope to be, is in all things and in all ways due to me!" When someone wants to give us advice, we rebel. Why? We are above advice.

2. *Being willful.* We want what we want when we want it, and we are determined to see that we get what we want when we want it! Alcoholics are known to be stubborn people. (Of course, other people besides alcoholics are stubborn, sometimes very stubborn.) This stubbornness is an outgrowth, or we may say an overgrowth of willfulness—of pride. We here put *our* will above others, when we really should be giving in to other wills. The positive side of willfulness is determination, which is valid provided that determination follows reason and value. Reason says we must follow a certain hierarchy of value in all of our actions; willfulness says to heck with values, we want what we want when we want it.

3. *Refusing to follow advice.* Seeking and following advice is an evidence of humility, because it is based upon the truth that we do not know it all and at times must seek someone else to help us solve our problems. On the other hand, the proud person does not seek advice because she does not admit to herself that she needs it. She knows all the answers; or so she thinks.

4. *Looking down on others.* This is so common that its examples are almost innumerable. We look down on others because they are of a different race or religion, or because we think them sinners or oddballs. Why? Because in our pride, we figure the ways they are different from how we see ourself makes them less than or below us. Pride tells us this. Whereas the truth of the matter is that we are all *equally* children of the same God no matter our race or religion or state of grace—no matter whether we're alcoholic or non-alcoholic, drunk or sober.

5. *Boasting.* Boasting is a bit different from "taking all the credit"—it's *adding* to fact. Instead of three years sober, we are three years and a half years sober. Adding to facts is boasting, and boasting is only our pride showing through in a little different way.

6. *Denying or minimizing our faults.* We see this sticking out all over in the holier-than-thou personality. You know the type: purer than angels but as proud as devils! The myth of perfection tells us that *all* of us have many faults and falls; humility, being truth, admits this to ourselves and to God and to others. How far above the proud saint is the humble sinner!

7. *Refusing to admit defeat.* This sign of pride is the cause of every disaster in history. It's an evidence of deep pride that's possessed by history's tyrants. Such people are very big cowards; they have no true courage, for courage itself is based on truth. It is never cowardly to admit it when we *know* we are whipped.

8. *Being weak in our faith.* When not stemming from an emotional condition, weakness of faith always comes from a cleverly shielded pride. But humility opens the door wide to a deep faith. Humility is truth; God is truth.

9. *Being fearful.* Here again we are not speaking of an emotional fear but of intellectual fear that is caused by some type of insecurity. This, too, is an element of pride looking for security in ourself. There is none. The truth: only God can give permanent security. We can take any example of the great human failures of history, and we can find many evidences of a great uncontrolled pride emanating from their personalities. Their pride directed all of their thinking and actions, and being based on a false assumption as all pride is, it led them to disaster. Think of the angels, the tower of Babel, the defeat of the Pharaohs, the Pharisees, Judas, Hitler, Mussolini, and on and on and on—even as you and I.

Pride remedy: Humility

We know that the one great remedy for pride is *humility*. But we also know that we cannot *think* ourselves into humility. We acquire humility, and thus minimize pride, only by a consistent and persistent effort. We do it by disciplining our thoughts and actions toward truth. Let's see two ways we can acquire this most necessary virtue:

1. *Meditation on the life of Christ* and other truly great people such as the saints. "Learn of Me," He tells us, "because I am meek, and humble of heart."[3]

2. *Meditation on the emptiness of fame and honor.* How fleeting and shallow are fame and honor.

Remember the story of the world's most successful businessmen we told in *Sobriety and Beyond?* It is so amazing and has such impact upon pride that it bears retelling.

In 1923, nine of the most successful businessmen in the United States held a meeting in a hotel in a Midwestern city. They were:

1. The president of the largest independent steel company—a millionaire

2. The president of the largest public utilities company—a millionaire

3. The president of the largest gas company—a millionaire

4. The greatest wheat speculator—a millionaire

5. The president of the New York Stock Exchange—a millionaire

6. A member of the U.S. president's cabinet—a millionaire

7. The greatest "bear" on Wall Street—a millionaire

8. The president of the Bank of International Settlements—a millionaire

9. The head of the world's largest monopoly—a millionaire

Here were nine men with perhaps the world's greatest accumulation of fame and honor and financial security. But in 1952, just twenty-nine years later, these same nine of the world's great and successful financiers gave the following almost unbelievable and amazing picture.

1. The president of the largest independent steel company—Charles Schwab—died bankrupt and had to live on borrowed money for five years before his death.

2. The president of the largest public utilities company—Samuel Insull—died penniless in a foreign land.

3. The president of the largest gas company—Howard Hopson—went insane before his death.

4. The world's greatest wheat speculator—Arthur Cutten—died abroad insolvent.

5. The president of the New York Stock Exchange—Richard Whitney—was prior to his death sentenced to Sing Sing.

6. The member of the U.S. president's cabinet—Albert Fall—was pardoned at prison so he could die at home.

7. The greatest "bear" on Wall Street—Jesse Livermore—died a suicide.

8. The president of the Bank of International Settlements—Leon Fraser—died a suicide.

9. The head of the world's largest monopoly—Ivar Krueger—died a suicide.

"Sic transit gloria mundi"—"so passing and empty is the glory that the world gives!"

Speak, History! Who are Life's victors? Unroll thy long annals, and say,

Are these whom the world called the victors—who won the success of a day?

The martyrs, or Nero? Spartans, who fell at Thermopylae's tryst,

Or the Persians and Xerxes? His judges or Socrates? Pilate or Christ?[4]

The reason that so many people who make their living in the public eye and whose success depends upon public acclaim, such as actors, must have that acclaim again and again and again, is that there is no human emotion more shallow and fleeting than public acclaim. For after the applause is stilled and the lights are dimmed, there remains only *emptiness*.

Recently an actor quit his profession precisely because of this fact. In so doing, he made a very pertinent remark: "It got so I could not stand it any longer. At one moment I was standing before hundreds of people listening to their applause; a few moments later, in my hotel room, I went in, closed the door, turned around, and there was nobody there!"

Pride remedy: Know thyself.

This remedy for pride is one of the oldest of the axioms of the philosophers. Nothing more surely brings us to the truth than knowledge of ourselves *as we are,* neither denying our bad points nor denying our good points. The person who works to overcome their admitted faults and who strives their best to use their God-given talents is the one least likely to be deceived by pride. "I am what I am!"

Pride remedy: Practice actions of humility.

This remedy specifies *actions,* because it is by actions alone that we achieve humility, and in turn control pride. What are some practical actions that lead to humility? Let's take a look:

1. *Obey all laws.* All valid laws come from the authority of God whether it be divine or natural, ecclesiastical or civil, regional or familial. Therefore, in obeying all valid laws, we are more and more striving to follow God's law in all things. And that is truth. And truth is humility.

2. *Cooperate with the plans of others.* This will go far in keeping the big "I" in its place.

3. *Occasionally refrain from giving our own opinion.* We do this just for the sake of practicing humility and controlling pride. But you know something? It really works!

4. *Practice frequent acts of kindness.* There is a vitamin pill called One-a-Day on the market. For spiritual well-being and spiritual health, and for a well-controlled pride and a well-founded humility, we could set up a spiritual one-a-day plan with very much profit. One act of kindness to someone every day gives us a conviction of being in *second* place!

5. *Accept humiliation and make them into acts of humility.* What is the difference between being humiliated and being humbled? There is a lot of difference. When we are humiliated, the truth has been thrust upon us against our wills; when we are humbled we have *accepted* that humiliation!

6. *Be grateful.* Not only should we say we are grateful, but we should *practice actions of gratitude* to God, our neighbor, our sponsor, our family, and all who have done good to or for us.

7. *Stay off the pedestal.* Deliberately take the back seat once in a while, just to control that pride! It might also be well to bear in mind that all humans find it difficult to balance on the pedestal. Alcoholics find it next to impossible; all find it impossible without a deep humility!

8. *Affirm our humility:* We might say to ourselves "humility is a sincere desire to be accounted what we really are" until it becomes a deep conviction.

9. *Seek God and His will in all things.* For this reason, the honest and sincere practicing of the Eleventh Step—"Sought through prayer and meditation to improve our conscious contact with God *as we understood Him*, praying only for knowledge of His will for us and the power to carry that out"—is the shortest and quickest road to humility and to controlling pride. In this writer's opinion, this is the core of the entire AA program. It is the essence of spiritual growth. It is the only highway open to ulti-

mate sobriety and, God willing, sanctity. A proud man will never tarry long on this step!

Pride comes from the Latin word *superbia*, which means "superb." Humility comes from the Latin word *humis*, which means "the earth." Could we not aptly wrap it up by musing: "Me superb? Hmmmm!? Let's come down to earth: I am what I am!"

COVETOUSNESS

Covetousness, the second of the basic passions, might better be termed "avarice." It is certainly easier to say, and quite accurate from its original Latin term *avaritia*. The English word *avid* also comes from this root. So we can define avarice as an excessive or inordinate love of money and worldly goods.

Avarice is not the same as envy or jealousy. In avarice, we desire the exact thing our neighbor possesses. We do not desire a duplicate of what she has, but *what* she has. Envy and jealousy, offsprings of avarice, might be satisfied with a duplicate; avarice would not. Let's take an example. We see a precious stone owned by someone else. We want it. We are envious of it. So we buy it, or we buy a duplicate. We have so far done no wrong. But if avarice goads us to get the stone unfairly or unjustly, or even to *willfully* toy with the idea of getting it unjustly, then it has gone beyond reason and law, and is wrong. Yet without this basic passion there would be no buying or selling; there would be no such thing as rare values. Nothing is worth much if no one wants it.

Avarice tends to lead us to possess not only what our neighbor has, but more material things than we need.

Then there is another kind of unjust desiring as described in the Tenth Commandment: "Thou shalt not covet thy neighbor's house; neither shalt desire his wife."[5] As long as the woman is married, there is no other way of desiring her but unjustly. And the same goes for the husbands being coveted by women! If this tendency in human beings was only *controlled in the beginning,* how many fewer divorces would there be in the world? But all humans by nature will *tend* to illicitly and unjustly desire what others have—goods and wives (and husbands). Because of the innate avarice in us all, the grass on the other side of the fence always looks greener; the other spouse is always more attractive; the other's cross always seems much lighter. Our job is to control this drive and prove to ourselves in mind and action the falsity of this "seeming" and the evil of its fulfillment.

The avaricious man or woman is always poor in the midst of plenty. Because like all of our passions, avarice feeds on itself and never can be fully satiated. He who gives in to avarice will continue to covet more and more and more and more.

We have an excellent example of this in the story in the Old Testament, which tells of the materially successful but avaricious man who exclaimed, "I will pull down my barns, and will build greater."[6]

But that night his soul was demanded. He had to render an account. He was weighted in the balance and found wanting. In worldly goods and wives? Hardly. But the spiritual vaults of his soul were empty, because those vaults are filled only by *giving,* not by *making and taking.* What we give away we keep and when we die we shall take with us *only* that which we have given away!

What are the evidences of avarice? Let's analyze a few. And we are going to use the word *tight* to mean common stinginess, which this writer feels the average alcoholic will better understand.

1. *Being tight even to relatives and the poor.* When this evidence becomes a reality in the personality, it shows a deep-seated avarice. For in most instances, the poor and relatives are the first to feel the pinch.

2. *Being tight toward yourself.* So many are not aware that skimping with yourself is an evidence of avarice. If this is indulged without any control, we end up with those who die apparent paupers but who in reality have much *wealth.*

3. *Being tight to the community in which we live.* We see this very frequently in ourselves and others. We so often excuse it as Cain did: "Am I my brother's keeper?" And avarice is the cause. Others excuse this tendency with another rationalization: "I believe in taking care of our own. Let others take care of themselves." Especially do we find this when the community is other than the one in which we live. Thus, it is commonly used to get out of giving "foreign aid." But it is all evidence of avarice.

4. *Being tight in driving a bargain.* The avaricious person always drives a hard bargain. They are slow to let go of worldly goods and determined to come out of every agreement a little ahead.

5. *Being slow in paying debts.* If we are unable to pay debts on time because we don't have the cash, but are honestly trying to be prompt, this is not a sign of avarice. But for those who can pay on time but don't, there is evidence of avarice.

6. *Being irked with slight losses.* The person who is a hard loser, who gets upset by unimportant losses, who walks away in a huff every time they lose had better take a big look at their avaricious tendencies.

7. *Being quick to criticize expenditures by a group to which we belong.* We see this in most groups. Whenever there is a motion to spend some of the groups finances, an avaricious person will immediately be on their feet objecting. Or have we done this ourselves?

Nothing makes the personality disintegrate more than avarice unchecked. It builds a higher and higher fence between others and ourself. This will come about unless we use some of the remedies at hand to control avarice and to cultivate its opposite: generosity. Let's look at some of these remedies.

Covetousness remedy: Meditate on the shortness of time.

Even with the help and miracles of modern preventative and curative medicine, human life, at most, is very short. Even if life would double in span, it still would pass so quickly. Everyone who has approached their later years knows this too well. This is not theory— this is a proven fact of the entire human race without exception. During a short lifetime, we have a very temporary abode. And whatever else endeavor, or talent, or Providence has given us—we can't take it with us!

There was a cartoon recently in one of the papers depicting a very elderly, emaciated-looking individual in bed. Beside the bed was a doctor. At the foot of the bed was a large pile of money. The patient was pounding the bed and the caption of the cartoon was: "If I can't take it with me, I won't go!" But you know something? I bet they did!

Covetousness remedy: Meditate on the length of eternity.

The saints were able to keep their passions under the control of reason by repeating to themselves and meditating on that very powerful axiom for spiritual growth: "Quid ad aeternitatem"—"what will this mean in eternity?"

Covetousness remedy: Remember money's inability to buy happiness.

We do not believe it is necessary to go into detail to prove this well-known fact. Although there seem to be very many who still try to prove it to themselves. Remember the nine successful men? It is a well-known truth that riches and happiness *can* go together; but they seldom *do!*

Covetousness remedy: Heed its results—lose friends, make enemies, be blind to reason.

A good example of this fact is the character of Scrooge in Charles Dickens's play, *A Christmas Carol*. He exemplifies all three of these results—he lost all his friends and became a very lonely man; he made conniving enemies; and he was completely blind to reason and reality.

Covetousness remedy: Realize that all things, material and otherwise, are from God.

Realization of the source of our material goods moves the will to gratitude and generosity. Getting the idea that *we* worked for what *we* have and that *we* were responsible for our material things leads to covetousness, stinginess, and all that comes in its wake.

Covetousness remedy: Practice liberality.

Another good one-a-day practice is to give just a little bit more than we had planned to give; or just a little bit more than we are obliged to give. It is sort of a loosening up of our muscles of generosity, which is a good panacea for avarice.

Now let's be practical. Let's see if we can enumerate some practical ways of using the above remedies. And to do so, let's stop a moment and think over a description from scripture. It is the description of the judgment, when the Lord is going to say the following:

1. *To the good:* "Come, ye blessed of My Father, possess you the kingdom of God . . . For I was hungry, and you gave Me to eat; I was thirsty, and you gave Me to drink: ... Naked, and you covered Me: sick, and you visited me: I was in prison, and you came to Me."[8] And, we are told, if we ask when we did these things, the Lord will reply: "As long as you did it to one of these My least brethren, you did it to Me."[9]

2. *To the evil:* "Depart from me . . . for I was hungry, and you gave Me *not* to eat; I was thirsty, and you gave Me *not* to drink. I was a stranger, and you took Me *not* in: naked, and you covered me not: sick and in prison, and you did not visit Me."[10] And once again: "As long as you did it not to one of these least, neither did you do it to Me."[11]

From the above has come a list of actions that are called the *corporal works of mercy:*

1. *Feed the hungry.* How few people seem to realize that two-thirds of the world's population go to bed hungry every night! Many, many people in certain parts of the world reach adult life without ever having had a really full meal.

2. *Give drink to the thirsty.* Thirst is one of the worst types of suffering. We in civilized lands on the whole have never really experienced thirst. But again, in many, many parts of the world, many people die each day from thirst alone! "I thirst!"[12]

3. *Clothe the naked.* There are many cities in this world of ours in which we can walk a very short distance before we see children and adults who are badly in need of proper clothing. How heartrending it is to walk in severe

weather and see so many suffering from a lack of clothing suitable to the climate! Or was that Christ unclothed?

4. *Ransom the captive.* Perhaps in modern life, this corporal work of mercy is not etymologically possible everywhere. But factually, it is workable anywhere. That is why the ones who work closely with the jail and prison groups are practicing literally this work of mercy, even though their success might not be up to the average outside. Remember? We practice the program for us. And even if there never was success with these men and women, what was it the Lord said: "As long as you did it to one of these My least Brethren, you did it to Me."[13]

5. *Harbor the harborless.* This is also a bit of archaic lingo. But it still means the same thing: see to it that someone who needs it gets a home, a place to stay. Oh, we know, there's no dues, no money in AA. But there are people, there are souls, there are a heck of a lot of the "My least brethren"!

6. *Visit the sick.* Physically sick, mentally sick, emotionally sick, alcoholically sick—there are thousands upon thousands of them all around everywhere waiting for someone to visit them. How easily we seem to sidestep this practice of visiting the sick. And yet how great the value, how effective the action! How close to Christ's heart!

7. *Bury the dead.* In many places people die and are left lie in the streets. But we also can practice this corporal work of mercy by attending a funeral, particularly the funeral of someone of the "least" and to which there probably won't be many other people coming! Nature urges us to give all the respect and attention to the deceased among those who are near or dear to us; but only fraternal charity will urge us to do the same for strangers or passing acquaintances, just as Joseph of Arimathea did it for Christ.

The corporal works of mercy are in reality the *giving program in action*. Remember? "This is a *giving program*." And where there is giving, there is little room for covetousness. For avarice is demanding. Like the rest of the passions, it is anchored in *pride*. The object of pride is *me;* the object of giving is *them*—the least of My brethren.

So before we leave the passion of avarice, let us for just a moment once more ponder: it is in the giving that we receive; what we give away we keep; and when we die we shall only take with us that which we have given away.

Never should we let our thinking and actions be motivated by the thought of how much we can get by with, but always by two questions: How much can I give; how great is the need?

LUST

Next to self-preservation, the passion of lust is the strongest in us. Although many confuse the terms *passion* and *lust,* lust is only one of the passions. Without it, there would be no human reproduction, and the human race would die out. It is *good in itself,* when controlled by reason and the laws of God. It is only when lust causes humans to break the laws of God or to go beyond the dictates of reason that it becomes sinful and so devastating in its results. The thought or action in itself is not sinful under the circumstances dictated by the laws of God and reason; it is only when it becomes a thought or action contrary to God's laws or dictates of reason that it is sinful and damaging. Everyone has lustful feelings, lustful thoughts, lustful desires, lustful imagination, lustful dreams. But these are not wrong in themselves. They only tell us one thing; *we are human.* Everybody is born with this tendency. And everybody will have this tendency until they die. It does not indicate that a person is terrible or different or awful. It is sinful only when we willfully entertain the thought or the desire or indulge in such actions *contrary to God's laws.*

Control of the sexual urge never hurt anyone—notwithstanding contentions by some psychiatrists to the contrary! But *repression* of the sexual urge has hurt very many misinformed people, because *repression* is the attempt to deny the very existence of sex and thus destroy consciousness of it. So it is that whenever a psychiatrist says that *repression* causes neuroses, he is correct, because the attempt to deny reality causes conflict and conflict in turn causes neuroses. Thus, the denial to ourself of the existence of any natural function will cause a neurosis. But *conscious control* never caused a neurosis, and this writer challenges anyone to produce a case where it did! In fact, control of sex—either by complete abstinence, or by moderation within the limits of God's law—rather than damaging the mind, on the contrary produces a sharper intellect and mentality. "My strength is the strength of ten because my heart is pure!"[14] "Blessed are the clean of heart, for they shall see God."[15]

Of course controlling the sexual drive halfway might cause anything! *Half-control* is the very essence of conflict! We are certainly not Freudian, and hence do not concur in the opinion that sex is at the bottom of all nervous, emotional, and mental troubles and problems. But we do feel that the modern trend to justify "half-control" is causing very many nervous troubles, particularly on a lesser intensity than an acute or chronic neurosis. After all, did you ever try to imagine what would happen if you placed a steak in front of a hungry man but always denied him meat? Yet the Trappist monks live their lifetime without ever eating meat, as also do many vegetarians. But they don't go around sniffing meat. Or have you heard the story about the Monk who, to make his penance more severe, tied a piece of smoked sausage in his room during Lent and each day sniffed it? What happened? He ate it on Good Friday! Now you make your own deductions about sex.

This writer agrees with the psychiatry practitioners who maintain that it is impossible to remain chaste or continent over a long period of time. But we would like to call attention to an omission. They left off something very important: without the grace of God! The drive of lust is so strong and such an intimate part of human nature that *it can be controlled only by the grace of God*. So it is not true to say we cannot control it, but rather that "God and I can *always* control it."

The very term for *lust* denotes that it is not absolutely necessary in the life of an individual. Lust comes from the Latin word: *luxuria* —a "luxury"! Something extra! And we define lust as an inordinate or unreasonable desire for or love of sexual pleasure.

In the matter of lust particularly, it is very necessary to differentiate between *ordinate* and *inordinate*. And to get a clearer understanding of this, it is best to go back to the story of creation and see that God created sex as something *good in itself,* and something very attractive in itself. Otherwise there would be no reproduction of the human race.

In the beginning, we are told, God created humans to His own image and likeness—He created the *soul* of human beings thus. But we are also told that God created us *male and female,* and that He told them to increase and multiply. Because of the burdens this would bring, He, in His wisdom and goodness, implanted in the act of procreation a most intense pleasure. So far so good. But we must realize that we were *first* created to God's image, which gave us the power of reason. Therefore, all else must be subject to this tremendous power God gave human beings and that He did not give to the lower animals, although He did give them the impulse and drive of sexual procreation of their kind.

Now let us take this a little bit further. When a man and a woman in lawful wedlock indulge in sexual relations to procreate their kind, *they become co-creators of a new human being!* Because God in his infinite wisdom and power produces along with their physical offspring a *soul, created (like the parents) to God's image and likeness!* What could be more beautiful? What could be more acceptable to the Divinity? What could be a more moral? What could be more normal![16]

But what happens? Humans, by our definition, *tend to indulge their passions, all of them, beyond law, beyond reason.* And when intellect and freewill concur in this tendency, there is sin; there is trouble.

So therefore to *feel* the urge of sex; to have lustful thoughts and/or desires enter our minds; to willfully indulge such thoughts or desires or to satisfy such feelings in *lawful wedlock* toward or along with your husband or wife is only normal, it is only human; but to willfully indulge such thoughts and/or desires or feeling or to satisfy them *outside* of lawful wedlock or toward others than your lawful spouse is contrary to reason and to God's laws, and therefore sinful.

Repression is also *inordinate*. Because reasons tells us we are human, that we are born with these natural urges, that we will be often conscious of them, but we can control them either through moderate indulgence in lawful wedlock or by ignoring them aided by God's grace in the state of continency. To deny their existence and to try to act as if we did not have such is neither reasonable nor healthy.

What are the evidences of lust in human nature? We do not feel it is necessary to delineate further on the existence of the drive itself. Everyone born of Adam is conscious of its experience. But what are the evidences that it is going beyond reasonable control?

1. *Pornography.* We find this evidenced in a preoccupation with all sorts of immoral pictures, magazines, and stories. The amount of this filth on the market is only an

indication of how far beyond reasonable control has the passion of lust gone in the modern world. 'Nuff said.

2. *Immodesty in dress.* And once again we find that the modern trend to downright indecency in dress is only an evidence of how far the passion of lust has begun to strangle modern civilization. Why do they dress this way? Ask them and they will tell you that they do it to look nice and to please others! Who is kidding whom? Whether they realize or admit it or not, they are following an innate instinct and drive to *attract sexually.*

3. *Lustful words, stories, or songs.* These usually emanate from the same mentality as pornography does. It is a mentality in which lust has taken over as chief pilot. In private conversation, in public statements—always the dirty story, the sexy innuendo, the crude remark. And once again behind it as with all the passions is *pride*—a childish desire to show off without an adequate mentality to do so. One time, a certain speaker was about to launch out into one of these crude stories, and with a feigned guilelessness, he slowly looked over the audience, and as he was doing so, he very naively remarked: "I just wanted to make sure there are no ladies present before I tell a story." Just then, from the back of the hall, came a very positive sounding remark: "There may not be any ladies present, sir, but you better remember that there are some gentlemen!" He didn't tell the story.

4. *Constant preoccupation with thoughts of sex.* This is not only an evidence of lust getting out of hand, but a very self-centered individual. Because *self,* as such, is very much intertwined with the sex urge and thus self-centeredness is bound to be constantly noticing this urge. Also a self-centered person always has as a byproduct of an overactive imagination, the manufacturing center of sexual thinking. Once again, pride is at work through lust.

So we have sex. So we have lust. And so we have many problems as a result. So what can we do about it? Let's see some of the remedies:

Lust remedy: Every form of self-discipline.

There is a saying, "If we can't beat them, join them." Perhaps we could use the same psychology with lust. "If you can't kill it, control it." And the basic way of doing this is through self-discipline. It is one of the indirect approaches to control of sex—of lust. All direct controls are dangerous because it is so strong. So is self-preservation. That's why we don't go around toying with our lives or our health. At least reasonable persons don't. All forms of self-discipline *strengthen* the will in matters of all the passions—especially the passion of lust. Therefore, we feel the first step in solving sex problems, either personal or social, is by teaching and practicing self-discipline, which alone plus grace will give self-control.

Lust remedy: Avoid the occasion.

This is the axiom growing out of the necessity of the indirect approach. This is one struggle in which it is never cowardly to run away or to retreat. Because there is no human will so strong that it can meet the drive of lust head-on and come out victor. This is a basic truth and the acceptance of it and practice of the avoidance of occasions accordingly is the only salvation from lust.

Again we might emphasize that we are not speaking of *denial*. We do not deny that we have the passion of lust. We freely admit it, accept the fact that not only does it exist but that it is stronger than any human will, and therefore we are going to avoid any unnecessary occasions that might cause this passion to be aroused.

Nor should we *fear* it. Fear of sex causes as much trouble as repression of it. In fact, fear usually causes repression. And many parents make a terrible mistake in instilling fear of sex into the mind of the child. There is only one way to teach children about sex and that is the *legal* way: *Tell them the truth the whole truth and nothing but the truth;* the simpler, the better, without fanfare, without mystery, without fear, tracing its origin as we did in the beginning—from God, by God and for God, so that we might, by use according to His laws and plans, become co-creators with Him. Remember? But *do* tell the child—or those other little boys and girls back in the alley will; and it won't be nearly such a nice or such a truthful picture!

Lust remedy: Emphasize the positive attitude.

Emphasize means to repeat and repeat and repeat. So again and again and again: *sex is something good, holy, natural, normal, beautiful, wonderful, and in its origin and proper use, divinely instituted.* God has told us: "Blessed are the clean of heart"[17] but He has not said, "Blessed are the ones without sex." "Blessed are the pure of heart" means, "blessed are they who use sex or do not use it according to His Will." By "heart," He means will!

Lust remedy: Keep busy.

When we went to school we learned the axiom: "Idleness is the devil's workshop." Be that as it may, idleness is certainly an open door to sexual thoughts and sex actions; and with that, the devil doesn't need a workshop!

The same is true of all the passions. The idle man is a pushover for them all. And what is more, all sorts of emotional difficulties and problems grow in the fertile soil of idleness. A hobby is a great restraint on all passion but particularly on lust, as it can gently push this particular passion out of the way.

Lust remedy: Accept it.

So many people have so much trouble simply because they will not accept such a thing as sex. They fight against its existence. They don't deny its existence, but are constantly resentful of it (or full of self-pity). As a result: tension, conflict, depression—more sexual disturbances than ever.

Lust remedy: Humility and blind trust in God.

Humility leads us to admit our powerlessness; trust leads us to depend entirely upon God for the grace and the strength even in the most violent passion. Our job is to do the footwork; admit our weakness; avoid the occasion; blindly trust in the wisdom and omnipotence of God.

ANGER

Without anger there would be little drive to action. For this reason the person of action is often the one who tends the more quickly to anger. The phlegmatic, the slow mover, the person of *inaction* does not usually tend so easily to anger. *Anger* controlled by reason is good, and even at times necessary and useful in maintaining discipline. But *uncontrolled* anger, anger that dictates action beyond reason, becomes wrong and leads to many troubles and sins. So it was that Christ Himself was *justifiably* angered by the money-changers in His Father's house, and in anger dictated by reason, He drove them out of the Temple.

Likewise the parent who is angered justifiably at the wrongdoing or disobedience of their children and *reasonably* and *with reason in full control* of that anger, justly punishes the child, is doing a *good* deed; they are practicing reasonable and therefore good discipline. But on the other hand, the parent who flies off the handle and then in anger that has shunted all reason aside whales the daylights out of the poor child, is doing wrong.

It is all very simple: *anger is good if reason controls it; anger is bad if it controls reason.*

The Latin term for anger is *ira*. So anger is always irritable, and is caused by some type of irritation, either real or imagined. We might define it as an inordinate feeling of displeasure at real or supposed injuries to us or ours, followed by a desire to unreasonably punish the offender or to fill up with self-pity.

So let us take a look at some of the evidences of anger in our human personality.

1. *Quarrelling—verbal or silent.* The angry man is one who is always getting into quarrels. Or perhaps he shows his anger by a cold, silent treatment. Instances where people do not speak to each other for days, months, or years are all evidences of anger. Many times in quarrelling and disputing we excuse ourselves by saying: "Well, after all I

am standing up for my convictions." But the funny thing is that a conviction is something we can defend without getting mad about it! And once again, anger comes along urged on by too much pride about us and ours.

2. *Cursing.* The most common expression of anger is angry words, and these often include curses. Incidentally to *curse* means to wish evil to someone or something. It is immaterial what words we use. Of course, when God's name is brought into the curse, it is much worse.

3. *Resentments, hatred.* Resentments begin in anger and feeling. Remaining, they may eventually become hatred —a matter of will.[18]

4. *Bitterness of speech.* Here all sorts of bitter language and/or remarks are evidence of an uncontrolled anger: sarcasm, cutting remarks, slander.

5. *Sulking or pouting.* Although in the alcoholic personality these evidences might be a manifestation of fear, still on the average they indicate anger. Likewise self-pity shows anger, for it is a resentment turned inside out. Anger seeks revenge; anger is frustrated in that seeking; so we have self-pity.

6. *Violence.* The person who is always making violent gestures of every degree, from making faces to shaking their fist, is expressing an explosive anger. In the same way, bodily aggression, fighting, violence of any type are all rooted in anger, which will always be with us, but which we *can* control little by little if *we* use the remedies.

Anger remedy: Anticipate anger.

Although it may at first seem irrelevant, on analysis expecting criticism and anger is one of the most effective remedies for anger. It is, again, accentuating the positive. We *will* get angry, so if we can anticipate these occasions with a prayer, a meditation of kindness, or a sidestepping of a situation, we will go far in controlling anger.

In *Sobriety Without End*, this writer detailed several gimmicks that are very effective in helping the alcoholic protect their ultrasensitive personality against irritation, especially in the early months of sobriety.[19]

1. *There is in every group of human endeavor at least one person who is against everything and everybody.* God puts them there to give all of the rest of the group a chance to practice tolerance, patience, kindness, understanding, and love. With this knowledge, it will be a pushover to ignore their diatribe. They are to be pitied, not blamed—certainly not to be an object of our anger. Such a fellow died. At his wake there was overheard: "Poor John, he won't like God!"

2. *Let the other person get mad!* We are in AA primarily to stay sober; secondarily to achieve and maintain happiness. Both sobriety and happiness are dependent on each other. We can't be happy unless we stay sober; we won't stay sober unless we are happy. Therefore when someone criticizes us, or talks about us, let them get mad—let the *other person* get mad for *he* is unhappy. All people who criticize or gossip or slander are basically very unhappy. Anyone who envies is unhappy. On the other hand, we want to be happy, so let's stay happy by letting the other fellow get mad.

3. *Words can never hurt us, if we don't let them.* And we won't let them if we are more concerned about what and how we are doing instead of what people are saying—for God alone can approve or disapprove, absolve or condemn. What was that saying we heard so often in our early school days? "Sticks and stones may break our bones, but words can never hurt us." Someone criticizes? Okay, what is that to us? Let them criticize, their words can't possibly change whatever we have done or are doing. Our lives and works are either good or bad; words can never change that.

4. *If we get a kick in the pants it can, only mean one thing—we are still in front!* All criticism is actually a boost. In fact, every knock is a boost. If our efforts were mediocre, no one would ever stop to criticize. A school boy by a slight misspelling said it a little differently but very succinctly: "Every knock is a *boast!*" He wasn't wrong at that. Get angry? How silly. Rather take a bow.

5. *Always do the best we can but never expect praise or gratitude.* A good conscience and the approval of God will be the never-failing result of the habit of looking only to God for approval instead of people. We can therefore shorten this gimmick: *don't expect from people!*

Anger remedy: Count to ten.

We certainly do not want to be adjudged facetious in giving this age-old advice, but it still ranks high to control anger. The Greek philosophers had even a more effective advice. They taught their offspring to recite the entire Greek alphabet before acting when angered. We feel such a therapy would enable even the most angry man to end up laughing!

Anger remedy: Know thyself.

If we are humble enough to admit to ourselves and others our true self, we will not be nearly so apt to become frequently angry. Angry at whom or what? Knowing us, we are no longer surprised at anything. Of course, we really should mention this remedy for all the passions, but to avoid repetition we won't, but we do remind ourselves that there are two remedies that are most effective for every passion: *know thyself* (which gives humility); and *prayer* (which obtains the necessary guidance and strength).

An honest inventory of our own shortcomings will go far in controlling the tendency to anger in particular. It will curb our tendency to strike back at injustices real or imaginary. And getting honest with ourselves will show clearly what is real and what is imaginary. For if we are honest we will more quickly accept all things in life more passively and more readily. It is something like the slogan suggested for safe driving on the highways: "Drive defensively." We could use that in most of life situations. "Live defensively." As the story goes, a fellow in tatters and rags, sitting on the curbstone, a little bit drunk, who was heard to mutter in a flash of honesty just as a very successful and wealthy person passed in a limousine, "There but for me go I!"

Anger remedy: Meditate on Christ.

Only once did Christ show anger—when the money-changers desecrated His Father's temple. In this, He was not only justified, but it was necessary to rid the temple of those He called "thieves." Throughout the rest of His life, he was meek and humble of heart.

In another incident in His life, we are told that, "Quievit"— "He remained silent." And again: "Nihil dicens"—"saying nothing."

Anger remedy: Practice smiling.

If this practice accomplishes nothing else, it will at least make everyone who sees us wonder what the heck we are up to! Then we challenge anyone to get angry with a genuine smile on their face.

Anger remedy: Daily acts of gentleness.

Here once more we have a one-a-day plan. Each day we go out of our way to practice actions of gentleness.

Many people foolishly begin each day with a resolution not to get angry. The very fact of this negative and repressing attitude many times leads all the more to anger. We begin by saying: "I am not going to get angry today." And we repeat it and repeat it—until finally we are so tense that it would be a miracle if we didn't get angry!

Anger is one passion that a negative approach only aggravates, whereas a positive approach will lessen the tendency, for example: an action of gentleness. Let's take a few more examples:

1. *Speak more softly.*

2. *Be quick to ask pardon.* (Not like Alphons and Gaston, but an honest "pardon me.") Remember the value of apology?

3. *Use kind words before anger.* Remember the age-old saying: "A kind word softens wrath"? You might even say: "A kind word beforehand stymies wrath!"

4. *Practice honest forgiveness of injuries.* If we practice forgiveness of injuries *no matter who was to blame,* it will still much anger in our heart.

5. *Meditate on the danger of resentments to alcoholics.* We feel most members of AA *know* the danger of resentments, but we fear many either don't let it become a deep conviction, or else don't realize that all resentments take root in anger. Control anger, and we shall never need to fear resentments.

6. *Take frequent actions of love.* Love not only casts out fear, but it casts out just about anything that is evil or tends to evil. But of course we are speaking of real love—not emotion. We fear that selfish *emotional* love in its frequent frustrations is but a wellspring of anger. But the love of the will—the love that sees God in all of His creatures doesn't have much room for anger. After all, God causes or permits all things, so if we want to get angry, to be honest, we should be angry with God. Or maybe we are?

7. *Pray for all people.* Honest, humble prayer for *all* people without any exception will be like a balm upon our soul minimizing all irritations and thus lessening the force and frequency of anger.

Many years ago, this writer worked for a hat company in Indianapolis delivering hats. One day while on a delivery, I passed the railroad yards and at their very edge saw a large crowd gathered. Being curious, I went over to see what had happened. There in the middle of the crowd lay a man dying. He had been run over by a switch engine. He had been cut in two but somehow was still living and speaking. But the only words that came from his dying lips were: "God, forgive everybody. God, forgive everybody!"

What beautiful last words. An echo of the Man on the cross: "Father forgive them!"[20]

GLUTTONY

For the alcoholic there is often much misunderstanding in the matter of the passion of gluttony. In fact, we fear that most people have a mistaken idea about gluttony in relation to alcoholism. We fear most people think that drunkenness—willful drunkenness—is sinful because of the excessive intake of alcohol, because the person has indulged in a sin of gluttony. Whereas actually willful drunkenness is a serious sin because in willfully getting drunk, the person gives up their use of reason without sufficient justification. The act of getting "drunk" is judged by its effect upon the individual not by the amount of alcohol imbibed. Excessive use of alcohol might be gluttonous, but many use alcohol excessively and do not get drunk.

In our present discussion of the passion of gluttony, we are only discussing the tendency within us all to eat and drink too much. Everyone tends to do this on occasion and we always will. But eating and drinking (any liquid, not only alcohol), and enjoying what we eat and drink within reason is *good*. Without this desire there would be no self-preservation. But overeating, and drinking too much is a tendency in all of us. And it also might be wise to call attention to the fact that drinking refers to.

The Latin word for gluttony is *gula*. Perhaps the reason behind this term is that it refers to anything that goes into the gullet. Be that as it may, we can define *gluttony* as an inordinate desire for food, or drink. And as with all of the passions, this desire is good in itself, and the pleasure of taste in eating and drinking has been put there by our Creator for our enjoyment. It is only when this desire goes beyond reason or God's laws that it becomes sinful. But we will all tend to do this and we can see evidences in this excessive desire in the following behaviors:

    1. *Daintiness, squeamishness in eating or drinking.* We see this whenever we see someone who seems never satisfied with the way in which their food is prepared or served. Or we see it in the person who is very particular as to the quality preparation of their food. One time this writer

had breakfast with a very important person. His order included eggs. But he sent them back four times until they were just exactly as he wanted them!

2. *Persistent overeating.* As we mentioned before, we all tend to occasionally eat too much, but when we habitually give in to this, it is evidence of gluttony. There is also an illness causing overeating—a pathology recognized by medical authorities. Such people have a compulsion to overeat that is very different from the urge of gluttony or even from a habit of overindulgence. It is pathological, and we find people suffering from this who actually die as a result of overeating.

3. *For Catholics only: Breaking the laws of fast and abstinence.* 'Nuff said.

4. *Eating solely for pleasure.* As we mentioned above, God has placed the element of pleasure in eating and drinking. It is there for us to enjoy. But we should also eat to live—not merely live to eat. The primary end of anything should never be excluded in its use. The primary end of eating and drinking is the preservation of the health and strength of the body.

5. *Excessive drinking.* Strange as it may seem, we find many more people who give evidence of gluttony by excessive drinking among non-alcoholics than among alcoholics. But here too, we must keep in mind that alcoholism itself is a pathology, and not to be judged according to moral standards.

Now comes a question that we know all members of AA will be very interested in—is excessive coffee drinking an evidence of gluttony?

First of all, it would be very difficult to reach a solid judgment as to just what is excessive. But even so, we feel that the coffee drinking of the sober alcoholic is not a moral problem, nor an evidence of the passion of gluttony, but simply a nervous condition picked up over the years and neither damaging nor immoral in any way. In certain instances, it may be damaging physically, but in these instances a doctor is to be consulted, not a theologian. So, have a cup of coffee on us!

Like all of the passions, when gluttony goes beyond the dictates of reason or law, then we need a remedy. Or better we should use the remedy first, before they go beyond reason's dictates.

Gluttony remedy: Fasting.

Not only does our Church prescribe fasting as a remedy to concupiscence, but doctors, philosophers, and teachers of all ages have advocated fasting as a very necessary practice in self-discipline, particularly in the matter of eating and drinking. And most doctors will tell you that eating and drinking too much is a causative factor, and a very important one in the ultimate breakdown of health and the early oncoming of old age. More people become ill from eating too much than from eating too little. Outside of certain areas of the world where people actually do starve to death, very few people become ill from too little eating. Of course in certain instances, the illness is from eating the wrong kind of food—only that which satisfies, instead of that which nourishes.

Gluttony remedy: Self-denial in other things.

Any action of self-denial, or self-discipline affects the total personality. Thus if we willfully give up legitimate things in life occasionally, it will not be so difficult to avoid the illegitimate when temptation comes along.

Gluttony remedy: Meditate on the fact that three-fourths of the human race go to bed hungry every night.

Living as we do in a land of plenty, it is very difficult to imagine this truth. Only meditation on it will convince us of its existence and in turn motivate us to avoid excesses of all kinds in eating and drinking.

Gluttony remedy: Look forward to our later years—to middle and old age.

We admit this is a very naturalistic motive, but any motive that is not bad is a valid motive. And if we are wise we will realize that our later years are going to be a time when nature will demand fasts of various kinds. Why not get into the habit? Many, many people find it impossible to follow the doctor's orders in regards to elimination of certain foods because they have never *practiced* fasting, which now is their diet.

The Christian idea of eating and drinking is very aptly expressed by Augustine when he says: "Whether you eat or whether you drink, do all things for the honor and glory of God and you have praised God."

ENVY

Like all of the passions, envy is a basic part of human nature. If this feeling were not present, there would be little motivation or competition in life. And envy, when reasonable and just, can goad us on to great heights to emulate another; goad us on to succeed as the other one has—but justly. But when it goes beyond the dictates of reason as it tends to do, and ignores the basic laws of God and man, it becomes evil and sinful, and leads to all sorts of sins and injustices.

Envy begins with a discontent with what we have, having noticed what others have or have achieved. So far so good. Jealousy enters the picture, and envy becomes unreasonable when we *resent* what others have but do nothing to compete, only doing what can destroy them. Under the guide of reason, we enter into just competition and may end up far ahead of the other person; but if resentment is the motive, we will seek to destroy the other one and only thus equal them. Unlike covetousness, which desires what the other person *has*, envy desires to get ahead of the other and to have *more than he has* or to become *more than they are*. We all tend to do this, and we all tend to do it unjustly, and beyond reason and the laws of fraternal charity—that is *envy*.

For every success in life, there are many people who, because of envy and jealousy, immediately set out to destroy what the another has or is achieving—by calumny, gossip, slander, and libel. This writer calls it the "penalty of leadership." Let's analyze it.

In every field of human endeavor, anyone who is a leader or is successful in a group must perpetually live in the white light of publicity where emulation and envy are ever at work. In art, literature, music, industry, and religion, the reward and punishment are always the same. The reward is widespread recognition; the punishment is fierce denial and detraction. When a person's work becomes a standard, it also becomes a target of the swords of the envious few. If their efforts and work be merely mediocre, they will be left severely alone; if they achieve a masterpiece, it will set a million tongues a-wagging. Jealousy does not protrude its forked tongue at an artist who produces a commonplace painting.

Whatsoever you write or play or sing or build, no one will ever strive to surpass or to slander you, unless the work is worthwhile. Long, long after a great work or a good work has been accomplished, those who are disappointed or envious continue to cry out that it cannot be done. Spiteful little voices in the domain of art were raised against Whistler as a mountebank long after the big world had acclaimed him an artistic genius. Multitudes flocked to Bayreuth to worship at the musical shrine of Wagner while the little group of those whom he had dethroned and displaced argued angrily that he was no musician at all. The little world continued to protest that Fulton could never build a steamboat, while the big world flocked to the riverbanks to see his boat steam by. The leader and the success is assailed because they who succeed *are* a leader, and the effort to equal them is but added proof of their leadership. Failing to equal or excel, the follower seeks to deprecate and destroy—but this only confirms once more the quality and the leadership that decriers are trying to supplant. It is the tribute that mediocrity pays to success.

There is nothing new in this. It is as old as the world and as old as the human passions—envy, fear, greed, ambition, and the desire to surpass. And it all avails nothing. Envy is usually sterile. If the leader truly leads, they remain the leader. Master-poet, master-painter, master-workman, and saint each in their turn is assailed, but each holds their laurels through the ages. That which is good or great or successful makes itself known, no matter how loud the clamor or the denial. They who deserve to live—live; eternally in their own work and in the hearts of the multitudes, they have inspired to imitation in maintaining their own niche in the masterpiece of the Maker.

The person who dares to live their deepest convictions and beliefs; to teach the ignorant the way Providence has given them to share; to face all controversy with a humble fiat but with an equally humble but firm and continued determination, that person shall be known as a truly great one on earth and in heaven. For they shall have followed closely in the footsteps of the world's greatest Leader, the world's most *envied* Leader; the world's most condemned Leader—Jesus Christ, who was assailed, called charlatan, scandalmonger, associate of the wine bibbers and the prostitutes; who was finally crucified by His own petty critics; and who was betrayed unto them by those nearest and dearest—but who now lives and will live forever in the bosom of His Father and in millions of human hearts, while his spiteful little enemies rot in the dust of forgotten history!

The penalty of leadership—the folly of envy!

Envy comes from the Latin *invidia,* which in its etymology means unable to see the truth, whence we so often say a person is blinded by envy. Actually envy is a jealousy or sadness over our neighbors' good fortune. It is, in plain language, a mixture of resentment, self-pity, and revenge! It is the direct opposite of fraternal charity: "charity envieth not."[21]

The Scriptures give us a specific case of envy at work in the life of Pilate, who we are told "knew that the chief priests had delivered Him up out of envy."[22]

Envy is the one passion of man that most easily brings malice into play instead of weakness.

Again from the Scriptures: "By the envy of the devil, death came into the world."[23] The devil envied man.

We feel that this passion causes more broken hearts, more broken lives, and more real damage to body and soul than all of the rest put together, with the exception of pride, because pride itself is the trigger of envy as it is with all the passions.

Let us look over some of the evidence of envy we see on all sides— including ourselves.

1. *A feeling of disappointment when others attain things or are successful.* This also is evidenced by resentments when others succeed. It leads us to be critical, then slanderous, then malicious, then destructive, and finally revengeful.

2. *Joy at another's difficulties, losses, etc.* "It serves him right!" This writer wonders if it is not a condemnation of our modern thinking in so far that laughter today is most responsive when the difficulties of another is portrayed. Maybe not, but I wonder.

3. *Indulging in calumny or slander.* The calumniator and the slanderer are veritable slaves to envy. They have not the first iota of fraternal charity in their hearts, and usually they are proud and arrogant individuals. Someone said: "Calumny is the attempt to step up by pulling another down."

4. *Backbiting.* This writer does not feel it is necessary to explain or analyze this very common condition existing in any group of human beings. But if we indulge in this questionable art, we better take a good look—our envy is showing.

5. *Persecution of others.* There are people in this world who have a persecution complex. It is actually their false pride. But in envy we speak of the ones who persecute *others*. The type of individual who is against anything and anybody. Their constant theme-song is belittling someone, persecuting someone. Their baton is envy.

6. *Always topping others.* These people always have a better story, a bigger this or a better that. No one can make any remark or do anything unless they claim they can say it or do it better—according to them. What was it we said: "*Invidia* [envy] means unable to see"?

7. *Bigotry.* Bigotry often stems from ignorance or misinformation, but it also oftentimes stems from envy. We criticize other humans because of their race, color, or creed because we are envious of that race, color, or creed!

8. *Gossip.* The omnipresence of gossip in the world is indicative of the widespread hold envy has on the human race. The ancient pagan poet Virgil wrote centuries ago "*Fama crescit eundo.*"—"rumor goes as it grows."[24] What a weapon for the envious!

Because envy is so widespread and is so damaging in the world, let us enumerate some of its devastating effects upon the world in which we live:

1. *Envy makes us mean and small.* Envy is often quick to take its toll, and a person who indulges it becomes very mean and small very quickly.

2. *Envy hinders our own efforts to succeed.* Success comes only to the person who concentrates on their work, not

on the work of their neighbor. "Age quod agis, et respice finem" is an axiom that has come down through the centuries: "Do what you are doing and keep your eye on the ultimate"—not on your neighbor's efforts.

3. *Envy alienates friends.* Envy being the opposite of fraternal charity, there is no room for true friendship in the envious heart. And since to have friends we must *be* a friend, by envy we gradually lose all of our friends and retain only a handful of "yes" me who in turn are very envious of us.

4. *Envy makes us unhappy.* The envious, ever anxious to supersede other humans, can never be at ease, can never be capable of love, and can never be happy within themselves. They are always being threatened by others.

5. *Envy ruins institutions.* The history of the ruination of various organizations, various institutions, is a history of the passion of envy beyond human reason and control.

6. *Envy destroys community efforts.* Nothing can be more destructive of community effort than the presence of an envious few who criticize and condemn every effort of the leaders, not because their efforts are misdirected or bad, but simply because these few who do the criticizing are envious of the leaders. And many community leaders give up, because they never realized that they must expect such envy in any concerted effort of leadership or responsibility.

7. *Envy drives us in on ourselves.* Unable to get revenge, the envious person turns their arrows in on themself and ends in a morass of self-pity.

8. *Suicide.* After self-pity comes loss of hope; and after loss of hope comes suicide. The final end of envy.

So—what are we going to do about envy?

Envy remedy: 1—Cultivate fraternal charity—to all people.

Herein lies the secret of all true spiritual growth; herein lies secret of all life's adjustments; herein lies the secret of the control of envy. We will not be envious of anyone we *really love*. But, we so often forget that love must be cultivated: practiced again and again and again.

Envy remedy: 2—Meditate on the effects of envy we have considered above.

We feel that many people are harmed by many things because they don't take time out to think over seriously the potential harm in those things.

Envy remedy: 3—Practice sharing.

We minimize envy by sharing our material and spiritual goods, our joys, and our sorrows.

Envy remedy: 4—Practice sympathy and understanding.

The one who is busy giving sympathy and understanding to those in need has little time to be envious. The person has acquired one of the finest habits and one in universal demand. So many today are in need of being understood, while so few are willing to understand.

Envy remedy: 5—Squelch rumors.

Even when we are successful in squelching a true rumor, we have accomplished a great deal and in turn are dealing a death blow to envy—both in ourselves and others.

Envy remedy: 6—Recognize this tendency in ourselves.

The quicker we recognize the envy within us, the easier it is to control it. It is when envy has been permitted to get a good hold on our thinking and actions that we will find it very difficult to extricate ourselves from it. "Resist beginnings, all too late the cure . . . ."

Envy remedy: 7—Pray for others' success.

Again, prayer is the universal panacea. But especially is this true in envy when these prayers are directed to God *for the success of someone we envy!*

Envy remedy: 8—Express wishes of success to others.

When good wishes remain in the mind, they are very often ineffectual and insincere. But if they are *verbalized* it is the old story of: "We can act ourselves into right thinking; but we cannot think ourselves into right actions."

Envy remedy: 9—Cultivate the friendship of God.

There is no room for envy or jealousy in the God-centered individual. Nor can we develop a true and close friendship with God and at the same time be envious of His providence or His children who are in reality and in truth our brothers and sisters, irrespective of the circumstances of their lives or the circumstances in which they live. It is a metaphysical impossibility to love God and to hate others! That means it just can't be done.

SLOTH

The tendency to "just sit and think" is in all of us. It is anchored in the passion of sloth. But if it were not for sloth, who would bother resting? It is only when this urge to inactivity interferes with obligations and responsibilities in life that it becomes unreasonable and sinful. But many of us all of our life will tend to just sit and think too much. (In fact there are some who would like to just sit.) This is the passion in man that makes getting up in the morning so difficult and that causes it to remain difficult no matter how long we have been doing it.

Sloth may be defined as an inordinate or excessive love of ease and idleness. Envy is disastrous in that it causes so many damaging actions; sloth is disastrous in that it causes the omission of so many *good actions* and obligations. We are also likely to ignore slothful tendencies, because through it we omit something and what we omit is not as disconcerting as what we *do*.

We see hidden evidences of sloth everywhere.

1. *Constant avoidance of physical effort.* As soon as there is work to be done, everybody disappears!

2. *Constantly looking for an easier way.* The saying that "many do more work getting out of work than if they had done the work" may not be so prosaic after all.

3. *Avoiding mental concentration.* There are three types of sloth: physical (avoiding physical effort), mental (avoiding mental effort), and spiritual (avoiding spiritual exercises, prayer, etc.)

4. *Distaste for spiritual exercises.* This is a evidence not only of low spirituality, but of a pronounced spiritual sloth. The spiritual life is a life—it is something living and, like all life, needs discipline and training. But sloth being in-

nate, the soul rebels against action and habit must be acquired through persistent effort. We are *not* born with a habit of prayer.

5. *Procrastination.* Spiritual writers refer often to procrastination as the "son of sloth." Well, son or daughter, it is a sure sign that sloth is at work!

6. *Inability to persevere for long.* The repeated beginning—giving up after a length of time; never being able to hold a line of effort or job for long gives evidence of sloth having a strong hold. The pity of this is that it often comes from childhood pampering by a doting parent.

7. *Habitual tardiness.* To this writer's mind, one of the most irritating (to others) of all bad habits. And although we feel that most times this habit is evidence of thoughtlessness, it also can be an evidence of sloth. After all, promptness is not innate; it takes effort.

8. *Neglecting obligations involving effort.* Here we will often find an otherwise well-disposed person, but the first obligations that are omitted are those involving effort. It is not malice; it is sloth.

9. *Wasting effort on useless things.* This comes about because effort with a purpose takes on the added burden of concentration and monotony. Doing a lot of things, but never much of anything, is not indicative of an active person but of a slothful person. We see this very often in the alcoholic, who, contrary to popular opinion, is very slothful. The alcoholic is always doing something, never accomplishing anything; always going places, a dozen or two at the same time! Much activity—little or no action. Action is *activity with a purpose.*

10. *Excessive self-analysis.* This self-analysis is indicative of a frantic attempt to find an excuse to get out of a certain obligation. Too slothful and lazy to meet and discharge their obligation, they turn in to find a reason why they

won't have to meet the obligation. Psychiatrists call it "retreat from reality."

11. *Gab-festing.* Endless talk without much rhyme or reason, thought or effort, sense or meaning. It is a beautiful cover-up of our distaste for real concentration and thought. Because of sloth, these individuals sidestep their own thoughts lest they see obligations that might involve purposeful effort.

12. *Spending more than normal or necessary time "in obliquo."* This, in plain language, means spending too much time in bed. Nobody likes to get up on time. Slothful people don't get up on time and most times just stay in bed.

As we mentioned above, sloth is often the cause of much disaster in life. So we will also, as we did in analyzing envy, take a look at some of the devastating effects of sloth upon the human personality and the world:

1. *Cowardice, fears.* Anyone who has indulged his slothfulness over a long period of time is a sitting duck for fear. Cowardice and fear are byproducts of an undisciplined mind. And an undisciplined mind is a direct product of sloth—mental and otherwise. We are not here speaking of emotional fear. There may be many reasons for such. But even in emotional fear, overindulgence of the nervous system and lack of discipline of the body opens the door for all sorts of emotional disorders, prominent among which is fear.

2. *Moral or social indifference.* No longer do we have to reply only on temptation or weakness to bring us to sin; indifference can do the same. It is the prelude to ultimate total moral corruption. An indifferent person no longer tries or cares; they are just plain indifferent to the laws of God, the laws of humanity, and the needs of those around them including their own family. The worst part about sloth is that it eats away the foundation of all moral life, by destroying the desire and ability of making an effort.

3. *Constant temptation to sin.* When the mind gives up effort, the imagination takes over. And when the imagination has taken over to such an extent that the mind no longer has much control, the imagination is always producing temptations of all sorts.

4. *Despair.* If we who have a well-disciplined mind and a well-disciplined habit of living, fall into sin—even serious sin, serious crime—we don't despair because we have maintained a habit of control. But when serious defection or serious problems of any type come along, the slothful person—the one who has slothful habits of thinking and living—has lost their control; despair is the result.

5. *Deterioration of civilization and nations.* Almost every other day there appears in our papers a question: "Do you think that America has become soft in its living habits?" Whom do we think we are kidding? We are following the path of the nations of history who achieved tremendous power and wealth by *discipline* and *effort,* and then proceeded to lose everything by lack of effort and self-pampering, by making things easier for everybody, and by giving everyone more aids to easy living and fewer lessons in self-discipline and survival of the fittest. In plain language, which so few seem willing to listen to, whether by indulgence or just plain sloth, nations *rot.*

If sloth is so dangerous to all, let's see what can be done about it. Let's take a look at the remedies for avoiding and changing slothful habits.

Sloth remedy: Practice duty—faithfully.

The basic point of army training is the habit of performing *duty first, last and always.* If we make duty paramount, we will not be likely to be bothered too much by the tendency of sloth.

Sloth remedy: Stop—think!

Centuries ago we were told the reason for the destruction of civilization: "With desolation is all the land made desolate; because there is none that considereth in the heart."²⁵ A disciplined mind is the foundation of all civilization. And the mind is disciplined by effort—to think; by frequent meditation on truth. Such will not only give us truth and the right path to travel, but also a well-disciplined mind that can prudently and wisely apply this knowledge. Education is not the acquiring of knowledge but the acquiring of a disciplined mind that knows how to apply the knowledge learned.

Sloth remedy: Set a rule of life.

We believe that it is because so many do not realize the power of passion, and in that we include sloth, that few people ever set for themselves a *rule of life*. This means having learned our limitations and our talents—that is what we can do; this is what we can't do. There is not much chance for sloth getting a foothold in such a schedule.

Sloth remedy: 4—Meditate on the passion of Christ.

Meditation on the passion of Christ is particularly effective in overcoming sloth. We cannot imagine anyone who thoughtfully watches the events of the first Good Friday permitting slothful habits to remain in their own life.

Sloth remedy: Practice—all for God and His Will.

Once more the practice of the Eleventh Step is very effective. What is God's will for us, that we shall do. In so doing, sloth may urge us to change, but grace will enable us to keep on going.

So there we have them—seven in all: pride, avarice, lust, anger, gluttony, envy, and sloth. Each one pulls on the soul in its own way; each one can be used for our sanctification or for our destruction. Let's see if we cannot find a digest of devices and practices that will ensure our salvation.

All remedies for the passions and for control of them can be reduced to three:

> 1. *Prayer and meditation.* This practice keeps at our fingertips the weapons necessary to subdue the *pride of life.* Searching out truth from the source of all truth, Almighty God, we hereby are enabled to see things as God sees them—to see ourselves as God sees us. And

thus knowing His will for us, are enabled by His grace to carry it out day in and day out. Seeing ourselves in the aura of grace, we will not be deceived by *pride,* but will ever humbly expect and get all things from the hands of an all-loving God.

2. *Fasting, self-discipline.* Herein we shall subdue the unruly desires of the flesh—lust, gluttony, and sloth. We keep the leashes that hold these drives in tow in good repair and strong. The strongest passion has little chance in a well-disciplined body and soul, aided by grace.

3. *Almsdeeds (giving).* The practice of giving subdues the desire to possess and rule. Avarice, anger, and envy cannot gain the upper hand in the personality who has established a solid habit of *giving.* We are not referring to the giving of obligation; that's justice. We are referring to the giving of the heart; that's love. To give and give and give—of our material goods and of ourselves just because others are all, without exception, children of God, even as are you and I.

Imprimatur.
✠ PAUL C. SCHULTE
Archbishop of Indianapolis
March, 1960

THE TWELVE STEPS OF ALCOHOLICS ANONYMOUS

1. We admitted we were powerless over alcohol—that our lives had become unmanageable.

2. Came to believe that a Power greater than ourselves could restore us to sanity.

3. Made a decision to turn our will and our lives over to the care of God *as we understood Him.*

4. Made a searching and fearless moral inventory of ourselves.

5. Admitted to God, to ourselves, and to another human being the exact nature of our wrongs.

6. Were entirely ready to have God remove all these defects of character.

7. Humbly asked Him to remove our shortcomings.

8. Made a list of all persons we had harmed, and became willing to make amends to them all.

9. Made direct amends to such people wherever possible, except when to do so would injure them or others.

10. Continued to take personal inventory and when we were wrong promptly admitted it.

11. Sought through prayer and meditation to improve our conscious contact with God *as we understood Him,* praying only for knowledge of His will for us and the power to carry that out.

12. Having had a spiritual experience as the result of these steps, we tried to carry this message to alcoholics, and to practice these principles in all our affairs.

ENDNOTES

1. James 1:12
2. Romans 7:19 and 24-25
3. Matthew 11:29
4. Story, William Wetmore, "Io Victus" poem, found in *An American Anthology: 1987-1900,* Edmund Clarence Stedman ed.
5. Exodus 20:17
6. Luke 12:18
7. Genesis 4:9
8. Matthew 25:34-36
9. Matthew 23:40
10. Matthew 24: 41-44
11. Matthew 24: 45
12. John 19:28
13. Matthew 23:40
14. Tennyson, Alfred, "Sir Galahad," poem, found in Poems (1842).
15. Matthew 5:8
16. (From original manuscript) For a thorough discussion of sex and sobriety, cf. *Sobriety Without End,* pp. 295-304.
17. Matthew 5:8
18. Doe, Father John, *The Golden Book of Resentments* or *Sobriety Without End.*
19. Doe, Father John. *Sobriety Without End,* pp. 185-186.
20. Luke 23:34
21. I Corinthians 13:4
22. Mark 15:10

23. Wisdom, 2:24
24. Stone, Jon R. 2005. *The Routledge Dictionary of Latin Quotations: The Illiterati's Guide to Latin Maxim's Mottoes, Proverbs, and Sayings.* Routledge: New York.
25. Jeremiah 12:11

About Hazelden Publishing

As part of the Hazelden Betty Ford Foundation, Hazelden Publishing offers both cutting-edge educational resources and inspirational books. Our print and digital works help guide individuals in treatment and recovery, and their loved ones. Professionals who work to prevent and treat addiction also turn to Hazelden Publishing for evidence-based curricula, digital content solutions, and videos for use in schools, treatment programs, correctional programs, and electronic health records systems. We also offer training for implementation of our curricula.

Through published and digital works, Hazelden Publishing extends the reach of healing and hope to individuals, families, and communities affected by addiction and related issues.

For more information about Hazelden publications,
please call **800-328-9000**
or visit us online at **hazelden.org/bookstore**.